WHAT THE BIBLE TEACHES

Original text material edited by William MacDonald

Developed by Emmaus Correspondence School
which is an extension ministry of
Emmaus Bible College
founded in 1941.

What The Bible Teaches may be taken as a correspondence course by contacting:

Emmaus Correspondence School
2570 Asbury Road
Dubuque, Iowa 52001-3099

ISBN 0-940293-21-8

234567890/4321098

Printed in the United States of America

TABLE OF CONTENTS

Chapter One

The Bible

INTRODUCTION

The Bible is different from all other books. When you see it, it looks like one book. But it is made up of sixty-six separate books, beginning with the book of Genesis and ending with the book of Revelation.

The sixty-six books of the Bible are divided into two groups. The first part is called the Old Testament and there are thirty-nine books in it. The second part is called the New Testament and there are twenty-seven books in it.

Near the beginning of each Bible you will find a list of the names of all the books in the Bible. It tells you the number of the page where each book begins.

WHO WROTE THE BIBLE?

At least thirty-six men had a part in writing the Bible. It was about sixteen hundred years from the time the first man wrote until the last man finished. But there is an important thing to remember. The Bible is inspired by *God.* What do we mean by the inspiration of the Bible? We mean that men wrote under the direct control of God. God guided them so that they wrote the very words that He wanted them to write. The following verses from the Bible clearly teach us that the writers of the Bible were inspired by God.

"No prophecy was ever made by an act of human will, but men moved by the Holy Spirit spoke from God" (2 Peter 1:21).

"All Scripture is inspired by God and profitable for teaching, for reproof, for correction, for training in righteousness; that the man of God may be adequate, equipped for every good work" (2 Timothy 3:16, 17).

So we see that the Bible *is* the Word of God. Some people say that the Bible only *contains* the word of God. This could mean that some parts of the Bible are inspired and other parts are not. But *every part of the Bible is inspired.* "All Scripture is inspired by God."

There is another important thing to remember. God has not given any other message to men. The Bible is the only written communication or revelation that God has given to us. In the last chapter of the Bible God warns us that we should not add anything to the prophecy of the book and we should not take anything away from it (Revelation 22:18, 19).

WHAT DOES THE BIBLE TELL US ABOUT?

The Bible has one main subject, even though it is made up of sixty-six books. The Bible tells us about Christ. The Old Testament told of many things that would happen when Christ would come. It told ahead of time something about His birth, life and death. The New Testament tells us about what did happen when Christ came into the world.

WHAT IS IN THE BIBLE?

The Bible tells us about the world from the beginning of time until the future when there will be a new heaven and a new earth.

The book of Genesis tells about the creation of the world, about how sin entered the world, about the flood, and about the beginning of the nation of Israel. The books from Exodus to Esther give us the history of the nation of Israel, up to about 400 years before Christ was born. The books from Job to Song of Solomon are full of wonderful poetry and wise sayings. The other books of the Old Testament, from Isaiah to Malachi, contain many prophecies, telling of things that would happen in the future. These books have messages from God to the people of Israel. God told them about their condition at that time and about what would happen to them in the future.

At the beginning of the New Testament there are four books which are called the Gospels. Each one of these books tells about the life that the Lord Jesus Christ lived when He was in the world. The book of Acts tells the story about the first Christians and about the life of the great Apostle Paul. The books from Romans to Jude are letters that were written to church groups or to individual men. These letters explain the great truths about the Christian faith and give us clear teaching about how we should live as Christians. The book of Revelation shows us the future. It tells us about the events that will take place in heaven, on earth, and in hell.

CONCLUSION

The following is what someone has said about the Bible: This book contains the mind of God, the condition of man, the way of salvation, the judgment of sinners and the happiness of believers. Its teachings are holy, its laws are binding, its histories are true, and its decisions are unchangeable. Read it to be wise, believe it to be saved and practice it to be holy. It contains light to direct you, food to support you, and comfort to cheer you.... Christ is its grand subject. Our good is its design. The glory of God is its end. Read it slowly. Read it often. Read it prayerfully.... It is the Book of books. It is the way God makes Himself known to man.

GROUP DISCUSSION QUESTIONS

Chapter 1 -- The Bible

1. Test your Bible knowledge. How many books are in the Bible? in the Old Testament? in the New Testament?

2. What is meant by 'inspiration' of the Bible? Look at 2 Peter 1:21 and 2 Timothy 3:17. Why is it important?

3. Describe some of the basic differences between the Old and New Testaments.

4. What are some of the general subjects that are dealt with in the Scriptures?

Chapter Two

God

The greatest thing that you can do with your mind is to study about God and your relationship to Him.

THE EXISTENCE OF GOD

1. The Bible does not try to prove that God exists. It just assumes all through the Scriptures that there is a God. The first verse of the Bible is an example of this. "In the beginning God created...." This verse presents God's existence as a fact that does not need to be proved. The man who says there is no God is called a fool in Psalm 14:1.
2. However, even apart from the Bible there are certain evidences to prove that there is a God.
   a. Men all over the world have always believed in a Supreme Being—One who is greater than they are.
   b. Everything must be caused by something or someone. The universe could not begin by itself.
   c. There is wonderful design and plan in creation and this means that there must have been someone to design it.
   d. Man is an intelligent being who knows what is right and wrong. His maker must be an intelligent being who is greater than man in order to create him.

THE NATURE OF GOD

1. *God is a spirit* (John 4:24). This means that God does not have a body. We cannot see Him. However, God can show Himself to us in a form that we can see. In the person of Jesus Christ, God

came into the world in a body like ours (John 1:1, 14, 18; Colossians 1:15; Hebrews 1:3).

2. *God is a person.* God has the same characteristics as we have. He knows and understands (Isaiah 55:8, 9). He has feelings such as grief (Genesis 6:6), love (John 3:16), pity (Psalm 111:4), jealousy (Exodus 20:5), and anger (Deuteronomy 1:37). He also has a will (Psalm 115:3; John 6:38).
3. *The unity of God.* The Bible clearly teaches us that there is one God (Deuteronomy 4:39; Mark 12:29). Read 1 Timothy 2:5. The teaching that there are many Gods is false and is contrary to reason. There can be only one Supreme Being who is greater than all others.
4. *The Trinity.* God is so much greater than man that no one could know what God is like unless God Himself made it known. The Bible teaches us that God is one Being but that there are three distinct persons in the Godhead, called the Father, Son, and Holy Spirit. These are not three Gods because the nature of God cannot be divided. We use the word "trinity" to describe three persons but one God. This is a mystery to the human mind. We cannot fully understand it, but we can believe it because God's Word says that it is true. We do not find the word, "trinity," in the Bible, but this truth is found in the following verses.
   a. At the baptism of Jesus. Read Matthew 3:16, 17.
   b. At the great commission. Read Matthew 28:19.
   c. In the blessing of 2 Corinthians 13:14. Read this verse.

   The Father is called God in Romans 1:7. The Son is called God in Hebrews 1:8. The Holy Spirit is called God in Acts 5:3, 4.

   The relationship between the persons called Father and Son in the Godhead is not the same as between a human father and his son. God the Father did not beget the Son in the human sense. Jesus Christ said that He was in the Father and the Father in Him (John 14:9-11). He said that He and the Father are one (John 10:30). This is not true of a human father and son.

THE NATURE OF GOD

It is difficult to explain what God is like. One of the best ways is to describe some of His qualities or characteristics. We call these the attributes of God.

1. *God is omnipresent.* This means that God is present everywhere at the same time (Jeremiah 23:24; Psalm 139:7-12).
2. *God is omniscient.* God knows all things. He knows all that we think and all that we do (Proverbs 15:3; Psalm 139:1, 2; Hebrews 4:13).
3. *God is omnipotent.* God has all power. He created the universe and now He controls it by His power. God is able to do whatever He wills (Jeremiah 32:17-18; Genesis 17:1; Matthew 19:26).
4. *God is eternal.* God never had a beginning and He will never stop existing (Psalm 90:2; Genesis 21:33; Psalm 102:26, 27).
5. *God is unchangeable.* God will never change because He is absolutely perfect (Malachi 3:6; James 1:17).
6. *God is holy.* God is absolutely pure and sinless (Isaiah 6:3). He hates sin and loves goodness (Proverbs 15:9, 26). God will not allow sin in His presence and therefore He is separated from sinners. He will punish sin (Isaiah 59:1, 2).
7. *God is just.* Everything God does is right and fair (Psalm 119:137; Daniel 9:14). He fulfills all of His promises (1 Kings 8:56).
8. *God is love.* It is God's nature to love (1 John 4:8, 16, 19). Although God hates sin, He loves sinners (Romans 5:8). Read John 3:16.

GROUP DISCUSSION QUESTIONS

Chapter 2 – God

1. According to the text, why is it difficult to believe that there is no God? Discuss some of the reasons (Psalm 14:1).

2. Does the Bible prove that there is a God?

3. What are some characteristics of God? How does He differ from man?

4. From all of the attributes of God, name some which would provide us with the greatest strength in times of need.

5. How does the fact that God knows all things affect our thoughts, speech, and actions when we are faced with problems or emergencies?

Chapter Three

Man

If we want to know the truth about man, we must turn to the Bible because "Truth is what God says about a thing." From the Bible we find out about man's creation, about his nature, about how he is related to other beings, about how he fell into sin and about what will happen to him in the future.

MAN'S BEGINNING

It is natural that we want to know where we came from. We have not always been here. Thoughtful men, called philosophers, have given different theories about man's origin. A theory is what someone *thinks* may be the reason why something happens, but it has not been proven to be true. The most modern theory about where man came from is the theory of evolution. Those who believe this theory believe that no one made man but that he developed from the lower animals.

But the Bible tells us, "In the beginning God created the heavens and the earth. . . . *God* created man" (Genesis 1:1, 27).

Why did God create man? God speaks of men as those "whom I created for My glory, whom I formed and made" (Isaiah 43:7). So we see that we were created to glorify God.

MAN'S NATURE

If you have ever seen a person die, you know that every man has a physical body and also a soul or spirit. At one moment the person is alive, and the next moment he is gone. His body is still there, but the life has gone. Only the dead body is left. Man is not only a body. He also has a soul and spirit.

The Bible teaches us that man is a three-fold being—body, soul and spirit (1 Thessalonians 5:23). It is hard for us to know the difference between soul and spirit because we cannot see them as we can see the body, but the Bible shows us that there is a difference. Animals have a body and a soul, but they have no spirit. A man has a body, a soul and a spirit.

The soul is what makes the difference between a living being and a dead one, but the spirit is what makes the difference between a man and an animal. Because we have a spirit, we can have a close relationship with God. Our feelings and desires come from the soul. Our ability to know and think comes from the spirit. Because we have a spirit, we are responsible to God. Our greatest duty is to find what God wants us to do and then do it.

MAN'S FREE WILL

God also created other beings in the universe. These are angels or spirits. They do not have a human body or soul. They are mightier than we are and they were also created to serve God. Like us they have a free will so that they can choose what they want to do. Some of them chose to disobey God and they fell into sin.

God could have made us like machines so that we would have to obey Him, without any choice. Instead of that, He made us so that we could choose to love and serve Him without being forced to do so.

MAN'S SIN

When God created free beings who could do His will or refuse to do it, He must have known that some would choose the wrong way. And that is what happened. There was a great angel called Lucifer, whom we now know as Satan. He decided to set His will against God. God immediately cast him out of heaven, as well as the angels who followed him. From that time Satan has been trying to stop God's plans in every possible way. God created man with a free will, and Satan planned to tempt him to disobey God. God had warned Adam, but Satan was able to make him sin also. We can read the well-known story in Genesis chapter three.

God, who is holy, is the ruler of the universe. He will not allow in

His presence any being who intentionally disobeys His commands. This is why God cast Satan out of heaven when he set his will against God. God did the same thing to man and drove Adam out of the garden and from His presence.

Every member of the human race has received Adam's nature. We are all born with a weakness or tendency to sin. It is easy for us to sin. No one has to teach us. When we are tempted, this nature responds and we yield to the temptation and sin against God.

MAN'S FUTURE

Just as the Bible tells us where we came from, it also faithfully tells us where we are going. Some day every one of us will stand before God and be judged. The fact of death is so common that we all understand that every man will die. But the Bible adds, "after this comes judgment" (Heb. 9:27). God has created us and has shown His will to us. God will surely hold every one of us responsible for everything we have said or done. In this life we are preparing for the next life. We do not die like animals. Our spirits must go to God, our Creator and Judge.

GROUP DISCUSSION QUESTIONS

Chapter 3 -- Man

1. Why did God Create man? Which of the attributes of God (listed in Chapter 2) were involved in the creation of man?

2. Define man as a three-fold being.

3. Why has God given man a free will?

4. As you look at Genesis 3, what were the steps in Eve's deception by the Devil? How does this help us to understand man's sinfulness?

5. What is man able to do in determining his own future? In this light, why would men rather believe in evolution than in God as the Creator?

Chapter Four

Sin

Read Genesis chapter three.

WHAT IS SIN?

As you read the Bible, you will realize that it gives very much attention to the subject of sin, what caused it and what can cure it. We often think of sin in connection with crime and murder. But in the Bible sin is anything that comes short of God's perfection. We read in Romans 3:23 that "all have sinned and fall short of the glory of God." When we think of the "glory of God" we remember that God is absolutely perfect. Therefore, if we are not being absolutely perfect, we are sinning. We are all guilty of this.

The Bible speaks of sin in the following ways:

1. Breaking the law of God, or lawlessness, is sin (1 John 3:4).
2. Fighting or rebellion against God is sin (Ezekiel 2:3).
3. Doing wrong is sin (1 John 5:17).
4. Moral uncleanness or impurity is sin (2 Samuel 12:9, 13).
5. Lack of faith is sin (Romans 14:23).
6. Neglecting to do good is sin (James 4:17).

Evil thoughts are sinful as well as evil deeds (Matthew 5:28).

WHERE DID SIN COME FROM?

Our first written record of sin tells us it took place in heaven. The angel Lucifer became proud and wanted to be equal with God (Isaiah 14:12-14). Because of this sin of pride, God cast Lucifer out of heaven. He became the one the Bible calls the devil or Satan.

The first sin on earth is described in Genesis chapter 3. It happened in the Garden of Eden. God told Adam and Eve that they should not eat the fruit from the tree called the "tree of the knowledge of good and evil" (Genesis 2:16-17). They disobeyed God and ate the forbidden fruit. And so they became sinners.

WHAT ARE THE RESULTS OF SIN?

1. As soon as Adam and Eve had sinned, they knew that they were naked, and they tried to hide from God (Genesis 3:7-10).
2. The punishment for sin is death. They became spiritually dead the moment they sinned. This means that they were separated from God—they were not able to enjoy God's presence. They also started to die physically. They did not die at once but their bodies were surely going to die later.
3. Every human being has received Adam's sinful nature. Every child that is born of sinful parents is a sinner by birth. Adam's oldest son was a murderer. Because we are all born sinners, we are all separated from God. We are all dead spiritually, and we will die physically some day. Read Romans 5:12-18 carefully now.
4. God cursed all of creation because of Adam's sin. This is the reason why there are thorns and weeds in the world. Genesis 3:14-19 gives us other evidences of sin. We do not need any other proof that sin is in the world as long as we have prisons, hospitals and cemeteries. Tears, sickness, sorrow, pain and death are some of the results of sin.

WHAT IS THE PUNISHMENT FOR SIN?

God has said that the punishment for sin is death. "The wages of sin is death" (Romans 6:23). We have already seen that this means spiritual death and physical death. This penalty must be paid. God must punish sin.

As long as we live in our sin, we are dead in spirit and our bodies will die some day. If we are still in our sins when we die, we will enter eternal death. This means that we will be separated from God's presence forever and will suffer in the lake of fire. This is called the second death in Revelation 20:14.

WHAT IS THE CURE FOR SIN?

God has given us a cure so that we do not need to suffer everlasting punishment for our sin. God sent His Son into the world to make a way so that we can escape. The Lord Jesus Christ was born of the Virgin Mary. He had no human father and so He did not inherit Adam's sinful nature. He was the only man who never sinned. He was willing to suffer the punishment for our sin when He died for us on the cross. He satisfied what a holy God demanded. Because the penalty of sin has been met, God will now give eternal life to anyone who confesses that he is a sinner and receives Jesus Christ as his Lord and Savior. (The lessons on the New Birth and Salvation will explain this more fully.)

When we trust in Christ, we are saved from the penalty and from the power of sin. This means that all our sins (past, present and future sins) have been forgiven. God will never judge us for them. We now have power to live for God instead of living for the pleasure of sin.

When you study about the forgiveness of sins you should remember that there are two types of forgiveness. The first kind is called judicial forgiveness (when we see God as a Judge). This has to do with the punishment for sin. The other kind is called parental forgiveness (when we see God as a Father). This has to do with restoring the fellowship (happy relationship with God) that was broken by sin.

When we say that all our sins have been forgiven—past, present and future—we mean the judicial forgiveness of sins. This means that the one who believes in Christ will never have to pay the penalty for his sins. This is because Christ paid the penalty for the sinner when He died on the cross. When the Lord Jesus died, all of our sins were in the future. Therefore He died for all of our sins. The moment we trust Christ as our Savior we receive complete forgiveness of sins as far as the penalty is concerned.

What happens when a believer sins? Sin breaks the fellowship between God and the believer. There is no longer a happy spirit of sharing or communication between the Father and His child. This fellowship will remain broken until the believer confesses that sin and stops doing it. The Bible tells us that when we do confess these sins God is faithful and just, and He will forgive us our sins and cleanse us from all unrighteousness (1 John 1:9). Here we are thinking about parental forgiveness. This is not a judge forgiving a criminal. It is a Father forgiving His child.

GROUP DISCUSSION QUESTIONS

Chapter 4 – Sin

1. Why does the Bible say that all men have sinned? Why do we avoid God's explanation of sin's existence?

2. What did Satan, Adam, and Eve have in common? Explain.

3. Suppose someone should say that all children are born into the world sinless as Adam was at creation, and that they do not become sinners until they disobey God as Adam did. Is this true according to the Bible?

4. How has Christ payed the price for sin? Why was He able to do so?

5. What are some of the feelings of a Christian who is out of fellowhip with God? How would Psalm 32 or 1 John 1:9 help in this situation?

Chapter Five

Christ

This lesson is about the Lord Jesus Christ. He is the central subject of the Bible. We shall learn about His deity, His incarnation (becoming a man), His work and His offices.

HIS DEITY

The deity of Christ means that Christ is God. The Bible clearly teaches that Jesus Christ is God in the following ways:

1. *The same words are used in telling us about God and in speaking of Christ.*
   a. He is eternal. Christ has no beginning (John 17:5; 8:58).
   b. He is omnipresent. He is with His servants everywhere (Matthew 28:20).
   c. He is omnipotent. He has all power and authority (Matthew 28:18; Revelation 1:8).
   d. He is omniscient. He knows all things (John 21:17).
   e. He is unchangeable. He is the same yesterday, today and forever (Hebrews 13:8).
2. *Christ does the same work that God does.*
   a. He created all things (John 1:3).
   b. He upholds the universe (Colossians 1:17).
   c. He raised Himself from the dead (John 2:19, 22).
3. *The same title is given to God and to Christ. He is called God.*
   a. God, the Father, speaks of the Son as God (Hebrews 1:8).
   b. Men called Christ God, and He did not refuse their worship (John 20:28).
   c. Demons recognized Him as God (Mark 1:24).
   d. Christ declared that He was God (John 10:30).

HIS INCARNATION

The incarnation of Christ means that He who is God came into the world as a man.

1. *The coming of Christ was predicted in the Old Testament.* Years before He came the Bible said that He would come (Isaiah 7:14).
2. *There are written records of the birth of our Lord Jesus Christ.* His birth was different from all other births.
   a. He was conceived by the Holy Spirit (Luke 1:35).
   b. He was born of a virgin (Matthew 1:23). He had no human father.
   c. Yet He was truly man. He had a body (Hebrews 10:5), He had a soul (Matthew 26:38) and He had a spirit (Luke 23:46).
3. *There are three reasons why Christ came in human form.*
   a. He came to show us what God the Father is like (John 14:9).
   b. He came to put away sin by becoming the sacrifice for our sins (dying instead of us) (Hebrews 9:26).
   c. He came to destroy the works of the devil (1 John 3:8).

NOTE WELL: One of the foundation truths that Christians believe is that Jesus Christ is truly God and that He came into the world as a man by the miracle of the virgin birth. As a man He was completely without sin.

HIS WORK

We shall learn about the death, the resurrection and the ascension of the Lord Jesus Christ.

1. *His Death*
   a. It was necessary for Christ to die (John 3:14). It was part of God's eternal plan (Hebrews 10:7). It was necessary to fulfill Old Testament prophecies (Isaiah 53:5). It was necessary to provide salvation for us (Ephesians 1:7).
   b. Christ died for others. He died in our place (1 Corinthians 15:3).
   c. The death of Christ was fully able to meet God's demands. Christ suffered all of God's judgment against sin. His death completely meets all of our needs because it was the death of a divine person. Therefore it has endless value.
2. *His Resurrection*
   a. It was necessary for Christ to rise from the dead. His resurrec-

tion fulfilled prophecy. It completed the work that Christ did for us on the cross (Rom. 4:25). His resurrection made it possible for Christ to begin His present work in heaven.

b. Christ's resurrected body was a real body. It was not a spirit (Luke 24:39). It was the same body that was crucified because it had the mark of the nails and the spear wound (John 20:27). Yet it was a changed body that could do things that our bodies cannot do, such as going through walls (John 20:19).

c. Christ appeared to some of His followers at least ten times after His resurrection. More than five hundred dependable witnesses saw Him after He rose from the dead (1 Corinthians 15:6).

d. The resurrection of Christ is very important. If Christ had not risen from the dead there would be no Christian faith (1 Corinthians 15:17).

3. *His Ascension*

   a. When Christ had finished His work on earth He was carried up into heaven (Mark 16:19; Acts 1:9).

   b. Christ ascended to heaven so that He might enter into His reward (John 17:5) and so that He might continue His ministry for His people (Hebrews 7:25).

HIS OFFICES

The Bible presents Christ as a Prophet, as a Priest, and as a King.

1. *As a prophet* Christ tells us what God has to say to us, and so He makes God known to us (John 1:18).
2. *As a priest* Christ speaks and acts for believers before God (Hebrews 4:14-16).
3. *As a king* Christ reigns in the hearts of those who are loyal to Him. In a coming day He will reign on earth for one thousand years. Psalm 72 describes how He will rule the world.

GROUP DISCUSSION QUESTIONS

Chapter 5 -- Christ

1. What are some of the ways the Bible describes Christ as being God?

2. How did Jesus Christ come into the world to become a man? How was He similar to men? How was He different from men?

3. How would he answer people who believe that there are other religions that provide other ways to God? How does your answer relate to Christ's words in John 14:6?

4. What is the importance of Christ's resurrection?

5. According to Hebrews 4:14-16 Christ functions as our High Priest before God. How does this give special meaning and encouragement in your life today?

Chapter Six

The New Birth

Read John 3:1-21.

INTRODUCTION

You have read in John chapter three about how Jesus talked with a very religious and moral man named Nicodemus. Jesus told him that it was absolutely necessary for him to be born again if he wanted to see or enter the kingdom of God (verses 3-5). It is absolutely necessary for each one of us too (verse 7).

WHAT IS THE NEW BIRTH?

Many people do not know anything about being born again and others have wrong ideas. See John 1:12, 13.

1. *The new birth is not the same as natural birth.* It is "not of blood." Your parents may be Christians but that does not make you a Christian.
2. *The new birth does not come by self-will.* It is not by "the will of the flesh." A child cannot will itself to be born physically. And just so we cannot be born again by our own efforts.
3. *The new birth does not come by human help.* It is not by "the will of man." No human being, even if he has a high position in the Church, can give the new birth to another person. None of the ceremonies of any kind of religion can ever give us the new birth.
4. *The new birth is not a physical change.* Nicodemus did not understand this but Christ showed him that it was a spiritual change (verses 4-6).
5. *The new birth is not a social or geographical change.* When a person

is born again, God does not suddenly take him to heaven. He continues to live on earth, but he now lives to please his Lord and Savior (1 Corinthians 7:20-24; Colossians 3:22-24).

6. *The new birth is not just knowing about it.* A person can be religiously educated and even become a preacher without being born again. We can know that the new birth is necessary and still not experience it.
7. *The new birth is not a process of growing and changing.* We do not slowly develop spiritual life in us. Sinners are dead spiritually (Ephesians 2:2). Life cannot develop when it does not exist.
8. *The new birth is not self-improvement.* It is not just getting rid of our bad habits. It is not a change in our way of living. It is a change inside of us.
9. *The new birth is not a religious belief.* We can be sincere in our religious convictions, we can be baptized and confirmed, we can join the church and take communion, we can teach a Sunday School class or be an officer in the Church, and we can even be preachers, and not be born again. Jesus was talking to one of the most religious, sincere, moral men of His day. He told him that even he must be born again.
10. *The new birth is a spiritual change* (verses 6-8). God is the only One who can bring this change into our lives (John 1:13).

WHY MUST A PERSON BE BORN AGAIN?

Jesus said, "Do not marvel" (verse 7). We should not be surprised that the new birth is necessary. It is perfectly logical and reasonable.

1. *We must be born again because without the new birth we do not possess a spiritual nature* (verse 6). The word "flesh" means the sinful nature that we received when we were born. If we leave off the letter "h", and spell flesh backwards, we can see that it means "self." When Adam sinned, his nature became sinful. Each one of us receives this sinful nature when we are born into this world. See Romans 5:12, 18, 19; Psalm 51:5.

   Romans 8:5-8 describes the character of this sinful nature that is called "the flesh." It is "hostile to God. It does not submit to (obey) the law of God." And so it cannot please God. By nature we cannot understand and enjoy the things of God or even desire them. See 1 Corinthians 2:14.

We can train "the flesh" and improve it and even make it religious, but we cannot change its nature. It is still rebelling against God and cannot please God in any way. "That which is born of the flesh is flesh."

The new birth gives us a new, spiritual or divine nature. Only when we have this new nature can we understand the things of God and enjoy them.

2. *We must be born again because without the new birth we cannot see the Kingdom of God or enter into it.* See verses 3-5. What does the "kingdom of God" mean? It is described as a spiritual experience. We read, "The Kingdom of God is not eating and drinking (physical); but righteousness and peace and joy in the Holy Spirit" (Romans 14:17).

   There are two kingdoms. One is called "the kingdom of men" and the other is called "the kingdom of God." One is called "the flesh" and the other is called "the Spirit." We all enter the kingdom of men by physical birth. We receive a physical nature that makes us fit for the physical kingdom in which we are to live. But how will we be able to see the value of the kingdom of God and enter into it? The answer is quite clear. We must have a new birth—a spiritual birth—that will put us into this new kingdom.

   Through this new birth we will receive a spiritual nature. This new nature will make us able to enjoy the spiritual realities of the Kingdom of God.

   Perhaps you have noticed in the margin of your Bible that the words, "born again" can also mean "born from above." This shows us where the new birth comes from. Physical birth is from *man* and the *earth.* Spiritual birth comes from *God* and is from *heaven.*

   Now read Romans 8:9. As God saw these people, they were no longer "in the flesh." They were "in the spirit." How did they get from one kingdom to the other? It was the work of the Spirit of God when they accepted Christ as Savior.

3. *We must be born again because without the new birth we do not possess spiritual life.* By nature we are "dead through trespasses and sins"; "alienated from the life of God"; "not having life." See Ephesians 2:1, 2; 4:18; 1 John 5:11, 12. A body without physical life is dead physically. A person without spiritual life is dead spiritually. Death means separation. If we are separated from

Christ, in whom is life, we are dead spiritually (John 1:4). If we are spiritually dead, how can we get spiritual life? Christ Himself gives us the answer. Turn to John 5:24, 25. If we hear the Son of God, and receive His word, and trust Him as Savior, we will receive spiritual life. We will be born again. See also John 3:16; 6:47; 10:26-28; 1 John 5:13.

GROUP DISCUSSION QUESTIONS

Chapter 6 -- The New Birth

1. The term 'born again ' has become very popular everywhere. According to the Bible, can you explain what the new birth is and what it is not? How is the term 'born again' misused and misunderstood?

2. What would one expect to see in the life of a person who claims to be born again?

3. Why is it impossible to understand the things of God without the new birth (Romans 8:5,6)?

4. What is the difference between 'the kingdom of men' and 'the kingdom of God'?

5. What are some of the differences between physical death and spiritual death?

Chapter Seven

The New Birth (continued)

HOW CAN WE BE BORN AGAIN?

Christ has showed us how we can have the new birth. Three things are necessary:

1. *We are born again by believing the Word of God* (John 3:5). In the Bible "water" is a well-known symbol for the Word of God. See Ephesians 5:26; John 15:3; Psalm 119:9. Here the word, "water," refers to the Word of God. It has *no reference to baptism.* From other scripture verses we clearly see that the new birth comes through the Word of God. See 1 Peter 1:23-25; James 1:18. When we read God's Word, it washes from our minds the wrong ideas we might have about God and His salvation. God's Word helps us to understand that we are lost (Romans 3:10-19), but that God loves us and has provided salvation for us (John 3:16). It shows us the way that we can be saved (Romans 10:1-17).

2. *We are born again by the Spirit of God living in us* (John 3:5). When Christ ascended to heaven, He sent the Holy Spirit, the third person of the Trinity. The Holy Spirit shows men their sin; He leads them to trust Christ. He gives each believer a new divine nature so that he can understand spiritual things. He guides those who have been born again into all truth. See John 16:7-15; 2 Peter 1:3, 4; Galatians 5:22-26.

   When we read the Word of God, the Holy Spirit convicts us; He brings the truth to our hearts. He shows us that as sinners we are lost, guilty, helpless and hopeless. He then shows us from the Word of God that we can be saved through faith in Christ who died to save us. The moment we trust in Christ, the Holy Spirit comes to live in us. His presence in us seals us, or marks us, as those who belong to Christ who has bought us (Ephesians 1:13; 4:30).

This is not a matter of *feeling* different, but it is a *fact* to be trusted or believed. We do not feel the new birth.

3. *We are born again by faith in Christ who took our place when He died as a sacrifice for us.* See John 3:14-16. Christ showed very clearly how this new life can come to sinners. Nicodemus asked, "How can these things be?" Christ used something that was written in the Old Testament to show how we can experience the new birth. Now read Numbers 21:4-9. Let us consider seven things about this illustration. Give close attention because this is *Christ's own illustration* of how the sinner can be born again.
   a. *Sin* (Numbers 21:5). Just as the people of Israel sinned, we have all sinned against God in what we think, what we say and what we do (Romans 3:23).
   b. *Judgment* (Numbers 21:6). Because of their sin they deserved God's judgment that came on them. God has shown His anger against all sin. See Romans 1:18; 6:23.
   c. *Repentance* (verse 7). The people of Israel realized that they had sinned. They confessed it and asked for forgiveness. They repented. Repentance is changing the mind, which changes the attitude, which changes the actions. God demands that sinners repent. See Luke 13:3; Acts 17:30, 31; 20:21; Mark 1:15.
   d. *Revelation* (verse 8). "And the Lord said." God showed Moses the way to save the lives of those who had been bitten by the snakes. God has shown us in the Bible His way of salvation for us (2 Timothy 3:15-17; Romans 10:8, 9).
   e. *Provision* (verses 8, 9). Moses made a serpent of brass and lifted it up on a pole so that everyone could see. Compare John 3:14. Just as Moses lifted up the serpent of brass, so Christ was lifted up on the cross, so that men dying in sin could look to Him by faith and be saved. On the cross Christ bore our sins. He took our place and endured all the judgment that we deserved because of our sins. By dying for us Christ satisfied all of God's demands against us as sinners. God showed that He had accepted Christ's sacrifice for us because He raised Christ from the dead. See Isaiah 53:5, 6; 1 Corinthians 15:1-4; Romans 5:7, 8.
   f. *Condition* (verse 8). "When he sees it." The serpent of brass was lifted up, but that did not save them. Each one who had

been bitten by the snake must *look* if he was going to *live.* Christ died for our sins and finished all the work that was needed for our salvation. But this will not save any sinner *unless he personally believes on Christ.* We must trust Christ as our own personal Saviour.

This is what our Saviour meant when He said, "Whoever believes in Him should ... have eternal life" (John 3:16).

Moses did not ask the people who were bitten to pray, or to pay anything, or to do good works in order to be healed and to live. So all a sinner can do is to look and live—to see his own need and trust entirely in Christ who died for him. He can receive Christ by faith as his own personal Saviour. See John 1:12; Acts 13:38, 39; Ephesians 2:8, 9.

g. *Result* (verse 9). "He lived." The one that the snake had bitten would surely die. But the moment he looked at the brass snake he lived. He received new life and it was as if he was born again. So a guilty, lost sinner can believe the good news that Christ died for his sins, and the moment that he definitely accepts Christ as his own Savior, he receives spiritual life or eternal life. The Holy Spirit comes to live in him and gives him a new nature. And so he is born from above.

This is the new birth that Christ said was absolutely necessary if we want to see or enter the Kingdom of God

WHEN CAN WE BE BORN AGAIN?

We can be born again at any time. The moment a guilty sinner looks to Christ and trusts Him as Lord and Savior he is born again. Why not do this just where you are? Stop trying to save yourself. Trust in the Son of God who did it all for you when He died for you. See 2 Corinthians 6:1, 2; Hebrews 4:7).

"Come as a sinner, and trust now in Christ,
Who bore your sins and shame;
Then by the Spirit of God through the Word,
You shall be born again!"

GROUP DISCUSSION QUESTIONS

Chapter 7 -- The New Birth

1. What place does the Word of God have in the new birth or in being 'born again'?

2. Jesus said, 'No one can enter the Kingdom of God unless he is born of water and the Spirit.' What is the meaning of the term 'water' as it is used in this passage (John 3:5)? Is it the same as baptism?

3. What part does the Holy Spirit play in our new 'born again' relationship to Jesus Christ? Can we understand the things of God without the Holy Spirit?

4. Is there a difference between feeling saved and knowing you are saved?

5. Have you experienced the new birth? Within the group, share your experience of coming to trust Christ.

Chapter Eight

Salvation

The subject of salvation is closely linked with the subject of the new birth. The new birth tells us the source and the nature of the spiritual life that all men need from God. Salvation includes the *results* of our deliverance and the *scope* (the great extent) of what God has provided for us in Christ. We shall think of seven things in connection with salvation.

THE MEANING OF SALVATION

The word, "salvation," simply means being saved from something. It is commonly used when a person is delivered from some danger. We speak of being "saved" from drowning, or "saved" from a burning building, or "saved" from a sinking boat. In each case three things are true.

1. The person to be saved was in danger of death.
2. Someone saw his danger and went to rescue him.
3. The rescuer was successful and delivered the person from the danger. He "saved" him.

The Bible uses the words "save," "saved," "Savior" and "salvation" many times. These words have the very same meaning in a *spiritual* sense as they do in the ordinary sense.

THE NEED FOR SALVATION

We need God's salvation for two reasons.

1. *We are sinful.* In lesson 6 we discussed our spiritual condition at birth. By natural birth we all receive a sinful nature, and so we are sinners by birth. This sinful nature produces sinful thoughts,

sinful words, and sinful acts. It makes us enemies of God. The Bible makes this very clear. Read Romans 5:12, 18, 19; 6:16; 8:5-8; Genesis 6:5; Ephesians 2:1-3; 2 Corinthians 4:3, 4; Isaiah 53:6; Jeremiah 17:9; Mark 7:20-23; Romans 1:21-32; 3:19-23.

These verses plainly show us that we are sinners by birth, choice and practice and that we need to be forgiven. We are lost and we need to be found. We are under judgment and we need to be delivered. We are guilty and we need pardon. We are dead spiritually and we need life. We are blind and we need to see. We are slaves and we need liberty. We are entirely helpless and we cannot save ourselves.

2. *God is righteous.* God is holy. He will punish sin. He will "by no means clear the guilty" (Exodus 34:6, 7). He has shown us His hatred of sin and He has passed sentence of judgment against all who die in their sins. This is eternal punishment away from God's presence. See John 8:21, 24; Mark 9:43-48; Luke 16:22-31; Revelation 20:11-15.

   Because we are sinners and God is righteous, we need to be delivered or saved from the penalty of our sins. Our cry should be, "What must I do to be saved?" (Acts 16:30-31).

THE PROVISION FOR SALVATION

The gospel is good news. Even though no one deserves to be saved, God has shown us His wonderful grace and offers salvation now to *you.* This salvation comes through His Son, Jesus Christ, because He died for you. The Bible clearly teaches us two things:

1. *Christ came to be the Savior of sinners* (Matthew 1:21). The Son of God is eternal and equal with the Father and the Holy Spirit. He became man so that He could provide salvation for you. Read John 3:16, 17; Mark 10:45; Matthew 9:12, 13; John 10:11, 15-18.
2. *Christ provided this salvation through His death and resurrection.* Christ was willing to die on the cross. He took your place and so He suffered for your guilt and sin. He bore your sins in His own body. All of God's judgment against your sin fell on Christ. He *fully satisfied* God's righteous claims against sinners when He died for you. God showed that He accepted Christ's sacrifice for you when He raised Him from the dead and seated Him at His own right hand. Read 1 Corinthians 15:1-4; 2 Corinthians 5:21;

1 Peter 2:24; Isaiah 53:5; Romans 5:6-9; Acts 4:10-12; 5:31; 17:31.

HOW TO GET SALVATION

All the work needed for your salvation was finished by Christ. What, then, must you do in order to experience this salvation?

1. *You must repent.* Repentance is simply a change of mind, that makes you change your *attitude* (feelings or thoughts) toward sin, toward yourself, toward the Savior and toward salvation. And this is shown by a change in your *actions*. Read Luke 13:3; Acts 17:30; 20:21. Instead of having no interest in salvation you will really want it. Instead of being proud you will become humble. Instead of being satisfied with yourself you will openly confess that you are helpless and without hope and that you deserve to go to hell.
2. *You must believe the gospel.* The gospel is God's testimony about the Lord Jesus Christ and what He did for you. See 1 John 5:9, 10. As a lost, guilty sinner, you must believe that Christ died for *you*—yes, *you!* You must believe that Christ took *your* place and died for *your* sins and finished all the work needed for *your* salvation (Romans 4:5).
3. *By a definite act of your will you must accept the Lord Jesus Christ as your own personal Savior. You must make Him the real Lord of your life* (John 1:12; Romans 10:9, 10; John 3:16; 5:24; 6:47; Ephesians 1:13). This is a very important act. Right now you may say from your heart: "Lord Jesus, I know that I am a guilty, lost sinner, but I believe that you took my sins on yourself and died in my place. I believe that there is nothing I can do to save myself and that you finished all the work needed to save me. I receive you now into my heart to be my own Savior. I make you the Lord and Master of my life."

   If you will do this, you will know what it means to "believe in the Lord Jesus Christ" (Acts 16:31).

HOW TO BE SURE OF SALVATION

How can we know for certain that we are saved? We can know because God has shown us plainly in His Word. God clearly tells us that anyone who trusts His Son is forgiven. He is saved and has eternal life. In Christ he is safe and secure forever. Read Acts 13:38; 1 John 2:12; Ephesians 2:8; 1 Corinthians 6:11; 1 John 5:13; Romans 5:1; 8:1; John 10:27-30.

THE SCOPE (THE GREAT EXTENT) OF SALVATION

Salvation has to do with the past, the present, and the future.

1. *The past.* We are saved from the *penalty* of sin. Because Christ endured the full penalty due to our sins, we are delivered from its dreadful punishment (John 5:24; Romans 8:1).
2. *The present.* We are also saved from the *power* of sin and from its *control* over us. At the time we believe, the Holy Spirit comes to live in us and He gives us a divine nature. As believers, we can enjoy deliverance from the power of sin in our lives (1 Corinthians 6:19; 2 Peter 1:3, 4; Romans 6:1-14). However, we are still able to sin. We still have the evil nature called "the flesh." But if we use the means that God has given us, sin will not have the first place of influence in our lives.

   If we want to be free from the power of sin, we must do the following:

   a. Read and study the Word of God and obey it (2 Timothy 2:15; James 1:22).
   b. Yield our bodies to God for a righteous and useful life (Romans 6:13; 12:1, 2).
   c. Always keep in touch with God by prayer (Hebrews 4:14-16).
   d. Immediately confess to God every sin we know about and try with God's help not to do it again (1 John 1:8, 9; Titus 2:11-15).
3. *The future.* Some day we will be free from the *presence* of sin. This will be when Christ returns. He will raise those believers in Christ who have died and He will change those believers in Christ who are alive so that they cannot die. This is the final part of our salvation that we are looking for (Hebrews 9:28; 1 Thessalonians 4:13-18).

THE RESULTS OF SALVATION

There are many results of salvation (Ephesians 1:3-14). We shall write down only a few of them.

1. *Peace with God* (Romans 5:1). We are no longer God's enemies.

2. *Acceptance as sons in God's family* (Ephesians 1:5; John 1:12; Galatians 4:5, 6).
3. *Joy in God as His children* (Romans 5:10, 11; 8:14-17; Galatians 3:26—4:7).
4. *Living for God* (2 Corinthians 5:14, 15; Galatians 2:20; 1 Peter 4:2-5).
5. *Service to God* in doing good works and telling others about Him (Ephesians 2:10; Matthew 5:16; Mark 16:15).
6. *Worship, praise and prayer* to God (John 4:23, 24; Hebrews 10:18-22; 13:15; 4:14-16).
7. *An eternal home in heaven* (John 14:1-3; Revelation 22:1-5).

May you give yourself no rest until you know, on the authority of God's Word, that you are eternally saved.

GROUP DISCUSSION QUESTIONS

Chapter 8 -- Salvation

1. Why does man need salvation? Do you believe most people realize their sinful condition?

2. How did Christ provide salvation by His death and resurrection?

3. What is involved in biblical repentence?

4. What is eternal security? How can a person have this security?

5. Are you pleased to think that you can have peace with God, acceptance into His family, and an eternal home in heaven? How can the knowledge of these things affect our lives today?

Chapter Nine

Grace

INTRODUCTION

All of God's dealings with us at the present time are based on His grace. This means that He shows us favor which we do not deserve.

The Bible uses the word "grace" more than 160 times. The New Testament mentions it 128 times. It speaks of God as "the God of all grace" (1 Peter 5:10). It describes Christ as being "full of grace" (John 1:14). It calls the Holy Spirit "the Spirit of grace" (Hebrews 10:29). So the three persons of the Godhead are closely linked with grace.

DEFINITION (MEANING)

The word "grace" as it is used in the Old Testament means to "bend or stoop down in kindness to someone who is inferior." In the New Testament the word "grace" means "favor, good-will, loving-kindness."

It is difficult to put in a few words all of the meaning of the word "grace." The following definitions will help us to understand it more.

1. Grace is love that is given to those who are not worthy. God is love; but when He gives that love to sinners who are guilty, unclean and rebellious, then it is grace.
2. Grace is God showing nothing but love and mercy when we deserved nothing but anger and judgment. It is God bending toward us in infinite love.
3. Grace was seen when God gave heaven's best to save earth's worst.

CONTRAST

Do not mix up grace with works. If we could get salvation by doing good works, then salvation would simply be our wages (Romans 4:4, 5; 11:6). God does not owe us anything. Salvation is a free gift.

Do not mix up grace with law. We are not saved by keeping the law. We are saved by grace.

Law gives us a work to do. Grace tells us that a work has been finished.

Law says, "Do this and you will live." Grace says, "Live and you will do."

Law says, "You shall love the Lord your God." Grace says, "God so loved the world" (John 3:16), and "We love because He first loved us" (1 John 4:19).

Law condemns the best of us (Romans 3:19). Grace saves the worst of us (Romans 3:24; 1 Timothy 1:15, 16).

Law makes us see our sin (Romans 3:20). Grace shows us salvation (Titus 2:11-13).

THE NEED FOR GRACE

We are sinful. We have disobeyed God's holy law (Romans 3:23; Colossians 1:21). Therefore we deserve only God's judgment. We stand guilty before the judgment bar of God because we have broken God's holy law (Romans 3:19; James 2:10) and so we are under the curse of God (Galatians 3:10).

Because men rejected and murdered God's Son, we do not have any claim on God at all (John 12:31-33; 3:18).

SALVATION BY GRACE

If we are going to be saved, it must be by God's grace. But God is holy. He will not overlook sin. Sin must be punished.

The gospel tells us how God can save sinners and how He can still be holy when He does it. Christ suffered the anger and judgment of God against sin. Because of what Christ did, God can forgive the sins of those who trust the Lord Jesus.

Christ has finished the work. Grace demands only faith from the sinner who seeks salvation (Ephesians 2:8, 9).

BLESSINGS THROUGH GRACE

Grace brings many wonderful results to sinners. The following are three of the greatest of these results.

1. *Salvation* (Titus 2:11-13). This means that the believer has eternal life.
2. *Justification* (Romans 3:24-26). This means that God counts the sinner who believes in Jesus as being without blame.
3. *Access to God* (Romans 5:2). This means that true believers can enter into God's presence by prayer. We are no longer separated from God by our sins.

GROUP DISCUSSION QUESTIONS

Chapter 9 – Grace

1. Discuss the meaning of Grace. Why does man deserve or not deserve God's grace?

2. Discuss the place of 'works' in the matter of salvation. Are works for salvation or a result of salvation? Explain.

3. Contrast 'law' and 'grace' and show the folly of trying to reach God by works.

4. Discuss as a group how you can demonstrate 'grace' in your everyday living.

5. Through Christ's death, discuss how grace demands only faith from sinners who seek salvation.

Chapter Ten

Faith

We do not study the Bible very long before we realize that faith is very important. We cannot be saved without faith (Ephesians 2:8, 9). Therefore it is important for us to find out what faith means.

WHAT IS FAITH?

Faith is personal trust or belief. We use the word in our everyday talk. We say, "I have complete faith in my doctor." We mean that we trust him to make us well. So, in the Bible, faith is personal trust in God. It means that we believe what God says and we trust Him to save us and to keep us.

WHERE DOES FAITH COME FROM?

If we look around us in the world, we will realize that some men do not have faith in God and so they are not saved. This makes us ask, "Where does faith come from?" In one sense faith is a gift of God (John 3:27). God gives us the power to believe on Him.

But how do we receive faith? We find the answer in Romans 10:17. Faith comes by what is heard, and what is heard comes by the preaching of Christ. It is the Bible that tells us about the Lord Jesus Christ. Therefore, if we do not have faith in God, we should read the Bible. As we read the Bible, we should pray something like this: "God, if this Book is your Word, if Jesus Christ is your Son, and if He died for me, then show me these things as I read the Bible." God has promised that if we want to do His will, we will come to know the truth (John 7:17).

WHAT IS THE OBJECT OF FAITH?

Faith must have an object to trust. This object may be a person, such as a relative or a friend. Or it may be something that is not living, such as a chair or an airplane.

It is not enough just to have faith. We must put our faith in a trust-worthy object. We may have faith in a motor car or truck. We may trust it to take us to a certain place. But if the motor is old and badly needs repairs, it may break down. Then we would find that we have put our trust in the wrong object.

The Bible shows us that the Lord Jesus Christ is the true object of faith (Acts 20:21). It is not so important how much faith we have or what kind of faith we have. The important thing is whether our faith is in Christ. If Christ is the object of our faith, then we are saved.

You can believe all that the Bible says about Christ and still not have faith in Him. In the same way you can believe that a certain train will leave the station at 11 A.M. and that it will arrive at your town at 5 P.M. You may believe all of the facts *about* the train. But you do not believe *in* the train until you get *inside* of it. It is only then that you are trusting the train to take you to your town.

You may know all of the facts *about* Christ and still not believe *in* Him. You may believe that Christ was born in Bethlehem and that He died on Calvary. You may believe that He rose again and that He went back to heaven. But you have not really believed *in* Him until you trust Him to save you from your sins and take you to heaven.

EXAMPLES OF FAITH

The Bible is full of examples of faith. In the eleventh chapter of Hebrews there is a list of many outstanding men and women who had faith. The Lord Jesus also met two people who had great faith. The centurion believed that Christ could heal his servant if He only spoke the word (Matthew 8:5-10). The woman of Canaan had a faith that was humble and would not be discouraged. She begged that the bread that belonged to the chosen Jews should be given to her (Matthew 15:22-28).

THE REWARD OF FAITH

God will reward true faith. No one has ever trusted God in vain.

God has saved every seeking sinner who has repented of his sins and who has put his trust in the Lord Jesus Christ. The Savior said, "The one who comes to Me I will certainly not cast out" (John 6:37).

GROUP DISCUSSION QUESTIONS

Chapter 10 – Faith

1. Define Faith. Define by examples how we exercise faith in our daily life.
2. Read Romans 10:17 and then explain how we can receive faith. Relate faith to hearing and learning to the word of God.
3. How is our faith in Christ superior to faith in a preacher, church or an organization?
4. Discuss an example of faith in the Word of God.
5. How does God reward faith? Read and discuss Hebrews 11.

Chapter Eleven

Heaven and Hell

Men have always had a great interest in the future. This interest makes us ask questions such as the following: Is death the end of everything? Where are those who have died? What can we know about heaven and hell?

WHAT HAPPENS TO US AT THE TIME OF DEATH?

From the start we must remember that man is a threefold being. He has three parts—body, soul and spirit (1 Thessalonians 5:23). We can see and touch the body, but we cannot see or touch the soul and spirit. With the spirit we can know God, with the soul we can know ourselves, and with the body we can know the world. Only God's Word can divide between the soul and spirit (Hebrews 4:12).

When we die, the soul and spirit leave the body. The body goes into the grave. The Bible describes the body of the believer as sleeping (Acts 7:59, 60; 8:2). It speaks of the body of an unsaved person as being dead. The soul and spirit never sleep.

If a person who died was saved, his soul and spirit go to heaven. Heaven is a place of happiness (2 Corinthians 5:8; Philippians 1:21, 23). If the person was not saved, his spirit and soul go to hades. Hades is a place of sorrow and punishment. In Luke 16:19-31 our Lord clearly teaches us that those who have died are conscious. They know what is going on. Be sure to read these important verses.

WHAT DO WE KNOW ABOUT HELL?

We have seen that at death the soul and spirit of an unbeliever go to hades. Hades is a place of conscious punishment (Luke 16:23-25).

Some of the earlier versions use the word "hell" instead of "hades." Hades is the correct word. The soul in hades is spoken of as a person. He had eyes, a tongue, ears, fingers and a memory. He had full knowledge of his condition in hades.

The Bible speaks of another place of suffering and torment in addition to hades. That place is hell, or the Lake of Fire. At the Judgment of the Great White Throne, the souls of those who are in hades will be joined with their bodies that will be raised from the grave. Then Christ will give the final judgment on the wicked dead. They will be cast into the Lake of Fire (Revelation 20:11-15). We may say that hades is like the city jail where the prisoner waits to know his sentence. The Lake of Fire is like the Federal Prison where a prisoner will stay for the rest of his life. When our Lord described hell, He spoke of the worm that does not die and the fire that is not quenched (Mark 9:43-48). Hell is a place of conscious punishment.

Is punishment for sin eternal? The Book of Revelation uses the words, "forever and ever," when it describes the misery of those who are lost (Revelation 14:11).

Can a God of love allow men to go to hell? God does not want us to perish. He provided for our salvation through the work of His Son on the cross (Romans 5:6, 8). If we reject the Savior, we will go to hell by our own choice. God is a God of love (1 John 4:8), but He is also holy (1 Peter 1:16). He will punish sin. We do not hesitate to put sick people in hospitals, or to put criminals in prison, or to put dead bodies in a grave. We can have love at the same time that we do these things.

What about those who have never heard the gospel? Like all other men they are lost sinners. Only Christ can save them. They can know that there is a God by the things that He has created (Romans 1:20, 21; Psalm 19:1). Their own consciences will also tell them that there is right and wrong (Romans 2:15). If they are obedient to the light that they have, God will give them more light. See the story of Cornelius (Acts 10 and 11).

WHAT DO WE KNOW ABOUT HEAVEN?

The Bible teaches that for those who know the Lord Jesus Christ and love Him, there is a place of happiness called heaven. The Bible uses the word "heaven" in three different ways. First of all, the region of the clouds is called "heaven" (Genesis 1:8). Then the area where the stars are located is called "heaven" (Genesis 1:17). Finally, the word "heaven" describes the place where God dwells. Paul calls this the "third heaven" and "Paradise" (2 Corinthians 12:2-4). We always speak of heaven as being "up." Satan said, "I will ascend (go up) into heaven" (Isaiah 14:13, 14).

We know that our Lord Jesus is in heaven today. After He was raised from the dead, He went up into heaven in a body of flesh and bones. He carried His glorified body into heaven. Read Luke 24:38, 39, 51; 1 Peter 3:22; Hebrews 1:3.

There are a great many believers in heaven. When a believer dies, he goes to heaven. The Bible says that he is "absent from the body and present with the Lord" (2 Corinthians 5:8). These believers are happy with Christ, "which is far better" (Philippians 1:23).

What is heaven like? The men who wrote the Bible could not find words that would describe it. In Revelation 21:10-27 the Apostle John describes the heavenly city—its foundations, its walls, its gates and its streets. They were all very, very beautiful. We know that in heaven there will be no sickness, no sorrow, no tears, no pain, and no death (Revelation 21:4). But best of all the Lord Jesus Christ will be there. We will be happy because we will be with Him.

GROUP DISCUSSION QUESTIONS

Chapter 11 -- Heaven and Hell

1. Define the body, soul and spirit of men as it relates to death of a believer and a non believer.
2. What does Luke 16:19-31 tell us about how we should live our lives while we have the chance?
3. As defined by the text, discuss Hades and Hell as relates to the unbeliever.
4. What about those who have never heard of Christ? Can they be saved?
5. What is the fate of a believer after death? An unbeliever? Where is heaven and what is it like? Is there a heaven now or is it something in the futue?

Chapter Twelve

The Return of Christ

The Lord Jesus Christ is coming back again. The New Testament speaks of His coming in two ways. First He will come to take His church out of the world. His coming for the church is called the Rapture because the church is to be caught up. Then He will come and reveal Himself as a mighty King to the whole world, which is called the Revelation.

Coming or Rapture

Several wonderful New Testament Passages refer to this first aspect of His coming. "When I go and prepare a place for you, I will come again and will receive you to myself, that where I am, there you may be also" (John 14:3). Jesus made this promise before He was crucified. Later the Apostle Paul reminded the believers in Thessalonica about the rapture. "For the Lord Himself will descend from heaven with a shout, with the voice of the archangel, and with the trumpet of God; and the dead in Christ shall rise first. Then we who are alive and remain shall be caught up together with them in the clouds to meet the Lord in the air and so we shall always be with the Lord". (1 Thessalonians 4:16-17) C.F. 1:10; 2:19; 3:11-13; 1 John 3:1-3)

When He comes all who have trusted in Him as their personal savior will be taken up to heaven. All who have His nature will go to be with Him. In Chapter six and seven we have already seen how to receive this divine nature. It is given to us by the miracle of the new birth when we receive the Lord Jesus Christ as our Savior. (John 1:12-13; 3:5-8)

After Christ has taken away those who believe in Him, there will be a time of very great trouble in the world. When the Lord

Jesus described it He said, "For then there will be a great tribulation, such as has not occurred since the beginning of the world until now, nor ever shall" (Matthew 24:21) It will be a time of such suffering that unless the days were shortened, no life would survive. (Matthew 24:4-28; Mark 13:5-23; Revelation 6:1-19:21)

At the time of the Rapture the Lord Jesus will come and the church will meet Him in the *air* (1 Thessalonians 4:17). He will not come to earth then, but at the time of the Revelation He will come to *earth* to reign. (Zechariah 14:4)

The Revelation

The time of trouble, will end when Jesus Christ comes down from heaven in power and great glory. (Matthew 24:31; 25:31; 2 Thessalonians 1:7-10; 2:1-12) He will appear as a conquering King. He will destroy His enemies and judge those who obey not the Gospel. Christ will then reign on earth for a period of a thousand years. (Revelation 19:11-21; 20:6) His 1,000 year reign is called *Millenium* a word meaning one thousand. (Isaiah 11:6-9; 32:1; 35:1-7; 65:17-25).

Following Christ's 1,000 year reign all unbelievers will be judged at the Great White Throne. (Revelation 20:11-15)

The earth will be destroyed. (2 Peter 3:10-13) There will be a new heaven and a new earth. (Revelation 21:1-8).

For believers the rapture is the next event to occur in God's plan. The Bible teaches we should live holy lives in view of His coming for the church. "Beloved, now we are children of God, and it has not appeared as yet what we shall be. We know that, when He appears, we shall be like Him, because we shall see Him as He is. And everyone who has this hope fixed on Him purifies himself, just as He is pure." (1 John 3:2-3)

Before the coming of Christ people will sin more and more. Some will even give up what they believe. "But realize this, that in the last days difficult times will come. For men will be lovers of self, lovers of money, boastful, arrogant, revilers, disobedient to parents, ungrateful, unholy, unloving, irreconcilable, malicious gossips, without self-control, brutal, haters of good, treacherous, reckless, conceited, lovers of pleasure rather than lovers of God; holding to a form of godliness, although they have denied its power; and avoid such men as these. But the Spirit explicitly says that in later times some will fall away from the faith, paying attention to deceitful spirits and doctrines of demons. (2 Timothy 3:1-5; 1 Timothy 4:1)

Are you saved? Would you be ready if the Rapture took place today? If you are a believer, are you living a life of holiness and fellowship with the Lord?

GROUP DISCUSSION QUESTIONS

Chapter 12 -- The Return of Christ

1. What does the text tell us about Christ's return?

2. After the Lord's coming for His church (Rapture) (1 Thessalonians 4:16,17) a great time of trouble called tribulation will come upon the earth. When will this time end?

3. According to Matthew 24:30; 25:31; Revelation 20:6, what will the millenium be like?

4. How do the passages in 2 Timothy 3:1-5: 2 Timothy 4:1 relate to the days in which we now live?

5. How should a believer in Christ conduct himself in light of Christ's coming again?

NOTES

NOTES

NOTES

NOTES

NOTES